#SingleSeason: Discover How To Be Your Best You While You're Single!

Paige Tucker

Copyright © 2019 Paige Tucker

All rights reserved. This book or parts thereof may not be reproduced in any form, stored in any retrieval system, or transmitted in any form by any means—electronic, mechanical, photocopy, recording, or otherwise—without prior written permission of the publisher, except as provided by United States of America copyright law. For permission requests, write to the publisher, at "Attention: Permissions Coordinator," at the address below.

Scripture quotations from The Authorized (King James) Version. Rights in the Authorized Version in the United Kingdom are vested in the Crown. Reproduced by permission of the Crown's patentee, Cambridge University Press

"Scripture quotations are from the ESV® Bible (The Holy Bible, English Standard Version®), copyright © 2001 by Crossway, a publishing ministry of Good News Publishers. Used by permission. All rights reserved."

Scripture quotations marked NLT are taken from the Holy Bible, New Living Translation, copyright © 1996, 2004, 2015 by Tyndale House Foundation. Used by permission of Tyndale House Publishers, Inc., Carol Stream, Illinois 60188. All rights reserved.

All Scripture quotations, unless otherwise indicated, are taken from the Holy Bible, New International Reader's Version®, NIrV® Copyright © 1995, 1996, 1998, 2014 by Biblica, Inc.™ Used by permission of Zondervan. All rights reserved worldwide. www.zondervan.com The "NIrV" and "New International Reader's Version" are trademarks registered in the United States Patent and Trademark Office by Biblica, Inc.™

ISBN: 978-1-7342946-0-6 (Paperback)
ISBN: 978-1-7342946-1-3 (E-Book)

Editor: Kendall Johnson
Front Cover Image: Terrol Henderson
Book Design: Be Your Best You LLC

Be Your Best You LLC
www.beyourbestyoullc.com

This book is dedicated to my Great Grandmother Catherine Ancrum Tucker (1930-2019). She always believed in me and encouraged me to be the best person that I could be. I am so grateful to have had in her in my life and am deeply blessed for the relationship that we had. I love you Grandma Cat! "To God be the glory!"

CONTENTS

	Acknowledgments	i
1	How Much Longer Lord?	5
2	Take One Day at A Time!	18
3	Use Your Time Wisely!	31
4	Enjoy Spending Time Alone.	41
5	Be Vigilant When Dating!	53
6	Don't Settle: Who You Want versus Who You Need!	66
7	Stay Ready and You Won't Have to Get Ready.	77
8	Understand That It Won't Always Be Easy.	89
9	Celebrate!	101
	#SingleSeason: Tool Kit	108

ACKNOWLEDGMENTS

Writing a book is much harder than I imagined. Of course, putting words on paper is the easy part; however, creating a work that will impact the lives of others is something that is different. It has taken me four long years to write this book and I have so many people to thank for making this happen.

First and foremost, I want to thank my best friend, Shannon. I remember when I first told her that I was writing a book. I had written about four or five chapters, and I asked her to read it for feedback. Not only did she give me feedback, but her reaction also inspired me to keep writing. She tends to speak her mind and tell it like it is. When she said that the words moved her, I knew that I truly had a good story to tell. I am very grateful for the time that she spent reading and providing genuine feedback.

Next, I want to thank my two friends, Ericka and Sabrina. They have been the big sisters that I never had. These two are always rooting for me and in my corner. There isn't anything that I have done that they haven't shown up to support. They have been shoulders to lean on and have encouraged me when I felt like I couldn't keep going.

I want to recognize my friend, Dennis for telling me to put my authentic feelings on paper. This was during my one-year rebellion when I was angry at God. I am grateful for his advice because it inspired me to write again.

To my family. To my uncle Kendall: for his editorial support. I am so grateful to him for being a positive role model in my life, being there when I needed him to be. I am grateful for his authentic feedback about how he was encouraged by the words of this book. He has no idea how this calmed my fears of whether this work would be good enough.

To my great aunt Theolanda: I can't thank you enough for always being there for me every time that I needed you. I appreciate all of the love and support that you have given me throughout my life. I thank you for being a positive role model and setting an example for me to follow. I hope I have made you proud. To my grandma Pam: thank you for your love and prayers. I love our long talks about Jesus. I thank you for inspiring me to live my best life as a single woman and being an example of what it looks like to not be shaken by life's circumstances. To my mother Candace: I thank you for choosing to give me life and for supporting me in all my many endeavors. I am grateful for the sacrifices that you made when I was younger to ensure that I had a better life.

I want to thank everyone who has ever supported me in any way. I am grateful for every customer, client, friend, and follower.

Lastly, I want to thank Jesus for loving me and keeping me during my darkest hours. I have never known a love so pure and unconditional. Without Him, I am 100 percent sure that I would not be here today. He is my friend, my comforter, my help in times of need, my hiding place, my place of peace, and my redeemer. I am grateful for every blessing, lesson, trial and tribulation that has shaped me into the woman that I am today. Without Him I am nothing. I am thankful to Him for loving me even when I am difficult to love. His love never fails and he never gives up on me even when others have. I can't thank Him enough for being who He is. I owe Him my life.

There is a time for everything and a season for every activity under the heavens
-Ecclesiastes 3:1 (NIV)

HOW MUCH LONGER LORD?

I walked across the stage to receive my master's degree and could not be more excited. I had just achieved another goal that I had set when I was 8 years old. As I walked back to my seat, I scanned the audience for my family and there they were, in the 3rd and 4th rows. I saw my parents, siblings, grandfather, aunts, and uncles. I saw friends, all there to support me, on my big day.

When I sat in my seat, my smile turned into a frown. I thought, "I'm twenty-six years old and just received my master's degree. I wish I had a husband to share this moment with." I would've given anything to have a husband, beaming with delight, that his beautiful and talented wife had just completed a milestone.

The truth is, there was no husband. I also had no prospects and it made me sad. Ever since I was a young child, I had always dreamt of what my future would be like. I am fortunate to have actualized many of those dreams. The only dream left was the one where I got married and had a family.

In the months leading up to graduation, I started to experience anxiety and frustration, because I was still single. I was in such a desperate state, that I started pleading with God to remove my desire for a husband and children because it was becoming too much to bear. I knew that he would not allow me to be tempted with more than I could bear (1 Corinthians 10:33 NIV); however, I had reached the point where I could not handle anymore.

I truly thought that the Lord would answer my prayer. I found myself bargaining with the Lord: asking Him to remove my desire, in exchange for a life dedicated to performing his works. My desire only intensified. I found myself crying myself to sleep in agony, constantly begging and pleading with him to remove this desire so that I could be more satisfied in Him. I finally cried out one night, "How much longer, Lord"?

The Lord answered me in silence. This added to my frustration. In turn, I spent countless hours reading articles about waiting on God to send my mate and what it meant to be given the "gift of singleness". As I read about the gift of singleness, I cried uncontrollably. As much as I liked gifts, this simply was not the gift I wanted. I was more than willing to wrap that gift up and mark it, "return to sender". As I cried, I always heard a still, small voice telling me that I would be ok. However, in the midst of my breakdown, I didn't want to hear that. All I wanted was for a God-fearing man to knock on my door and whisk me away. If I'm being honest, I knew that was not going to happen.

I disabled my social media because I was tired of seeing others share the happiness of their engagements, marriages, and children. I wanted to be one of those people. Again, I asked, "How much longer, Lord"? Still, there was no answer. This feeling had become all too familiar for me. I had not been very successful in the love department. I spent much more time being single than I had been in a relationship. Every relationship I had been in ended in complete heartbreak. The longest relationship I had been in was one week shy of a year.

People have always told me that I am so awesome. "You will make a great wife and an awesome mother", were often things that I heard. I often found myself thinking: "If men think that I am so awesome, why do they continue to overlook me, and why in the world am I not married?" At twenty-six, I had only had five "official" boyfriends, in my entire life and only two in my adult life. It seemed that I only could get men who I was unequally yoked with. The ones who had the qualities that I looked for always wanted to date me, but never commit.

This was exhausting. I was tired of being disappointed and feeling like I was being passed over. These feelings did a number on my self-esteem and I naturally started to ask the question, "what is wrong with me?" I started to feel like my eight-year-old self, who had been bullied for physical attributes beyond my control. I felt so ugly.

Despite these feelings, I decided that I was going to make the most of my singleness. I put my prayer for a husband to God on hold and started focusing on other things. To occupy my time, I started participating in various things in my community. I volunteered with the homeless, food pantries, and non-profits that helped those living in poverty. I found this to be rewarding.

I also found myself getting closer to God. I started reading daily devotionals, hosting a small group, and spending more time in prayer. I found this to be working. I also spent more time traveling. My job afforded me the opportunity to travel every few months. This seemed to be fulfilling until I decided to reactivate my social media. Oh, why did I do that? Once again, I started to feel the urge to have a husband and start a family. I even asked some friends to hook me up with someone. They did introduce me to someone and he was everything I thought I needed in someone but I did feel some apprehension. He also did not seem to be interested, so once again I was a little sad. I did pray to God about it one time, but I don't think I waited long enough for an answer.

Before God could give me an answer, my ex reached out to me. I was taken aback when I saw his name on my phone because I had not heard from him in almost two years. There were no texts, phone calls, social media messages, or anything of the sort. I responded to him cordially and then that is when he started talking about how much he still loved me and wanted to be with me. I thought it was a joke.

However, I was frustrated because I couldn't believe that he thought it would be that easy to come back into my life, after the way that he had hurt me. I told him that while I had forgiven him for the violations in the past, it was best we no longer spoke. Ironically, I did wish him the best. I believed that this was the last time that I would hear from him. I quickly forgot about the encounter and went on with my life.

Over the next couple of months, I continued to occupy myself with church and volunteer work. Two months later, my ex contacted me again. This time I spoke with him over the phone and we started to talk more frequently. Then, we started hanging out and quickly revisited the idea of being back in love with each other.

To my surprise, not only did we fall in love again, we started going to church together, as well as going on adventures on the weekends. We soon decided that we would get married, at the end of the year. I was beyond excited. I thought that God had answered my prayer, by giving me a husband. He didn't give me just any husband, he gave me a man that I had once loved deeply, and one that I loved even more now. We discussed getting engaged and then moving in together, before getting married.

We did end up moving in together; unsurprisingly, the engagement did not happen. I admit this changed my attitude towards the relationship. I was disappointed that we, once again, were at this place of uncertainty. I can only blame myself, for not sticking to the promise I made, to myself, not to live with someone before we were engaged to be married.

When I look back on my past, I now know that I don't want to live with anyone until we have said the words "I do." Not only did the relationship suffer, so did my relationship with God. The main problem was that the man I was in love with did not have a strong relationship with God. I found myself being torn between God and my relationship.

The enemy also started to reveal himself in the relationship as I realized that this relationship was not from God but simply a counterfeit. After much turmoil, the relationship came to an end. I must admit, it was the first time I was ever happy to be single.

I finally decided to embrace my singleness. I thought to myself, why not make the most of this? I realized that being in a relationship took away from the time that I spent with God. I remembered what Paul said about singleness being better because the married woman can find herself choosing between spending time with her husband and serving God (1Cor.7:34-35 NIV). I admit that my attitude toward singleness changes, based on where I am in my life.

For some reason, the beginning of each year is the hardest for me. It is usually during the new year that I get anxious and depressed that my situation has not changed.

There are days that I wonder if this single season will ever end, having endured it for so long. I often joke that Jesus will come back before I get into a lasting relationship. Honestly, as time passes, it seems that the joke is turning into a reality. I know that God has me here for a reason however I admit it is hard. As I continue to reflect, I realize that, while I remained in this season, there was still work that I needed to do to prepare for my next season in life. Even if God doesn't send me someone, at least I know I have done the work needed to become the best version of myself.

I started writing this book four years ago. I had been trying to avoid finishing it because I did not want to be the poster child for singleness. However, when God wants something done, He will keep you in a certain season until His will is done. This reminds me of the Israelites being in the wilderness for 40 years, due to their doubt and unbelief. God never intended for them to be there that long. Unfortunately, they didn't believe His promises, therefore, they were delayed from inheriting the Promised Land (Numbers 14).

I had to have a long and hard conversation with myself to understand that completing this book is so much more than me. I needed to get over myself to share the gift that God has given me. Due to this internal struggle, you will notice that the tone of the book changes. This is to represent the shifts in my life. I wanted to be transparent and authentic with you because I know that being single is not always easy. I wanted this book to reflect what we experience, during our single journey.

While I will discuss relationships, this book was created to help you become the best version of yourself, in this season of singleness. Each chapter ends with either a challenge for you to complete or some questions for self-reflection. The main objective of these challenges is for you to walk away with practical ways to be your best you, while you are in your single season. I also encourage you to utilize the reflection sections found at the end of each chapter. I pray that this book changes your life, encourages you to be your best and that it blesses you beyond measure.

SELF-REFLECTION:

1. What do you expect to get out of reading this book?
2. What has your single season been like thus far?
3. Are you ready for your single season to be over?
4. What do you need to work on to become the best version of yourself?

INTROSPECTION

_____
_____
_____
_____
_____
_____
_____
_____

HOW MUCH LONGER LORD?

#SINGLE SEASON: DISCOVER HOW TO BE YOUR BEST YOU'RE WHILE SINGLE

HOW MUCH LONGER LORD?

TAKE ONE DAY AT A TIME

One of my greatest flaws is that I worry about the future. Not only do I worry about the future, but I also create a whole new reality based on what I think will happen. Many times, these things never come to pass, and I end up wasting a great deal of time in the present because I'm so focused on the future. My pastor once preached a sermon about depression. He talked about how we worry about things that never happen, and he used Elijah as a great example. Elijah spent a great deal of time worried about dying. He even ran away from Jezebel trying to escape death.

However, he greatly underestimated the Lord and His grace. Not only did Jezebel not kill Elijah, he never died. He was carried away into heaven by a chariot of fire. 2 Kings 2:11 says, *as they were walking along and talking together, suddenly a chariot of fire and horses of fire appeared and separated the two of them, and Elijah went up to heaven in a whirlwind (NIV)*. God remembered Elijah's faithfulness and He rewarded him for it. I also want you to look at the way Elijah's life changed in a moment's notice. He was walking along talking with Elisha and in the next breath, he was whisked away to Heaven.

I used this example to remind you not to spend the valuable time that you have been blessed with, worrying about your future and what may happen. The Lord can drastically change your life in a moment's notice, and then you could realize the many things you missed out on, in the present, because you were so worried about what could happen instead of what is happening.

This is not to say that you shouldn't contemplate your future or accomplish things that may set you up for a better future. For instance, advancing my career and education are important to me. So, I focused on those things, instead of dating someone. Spending long waking nights worrying about whether or not the Lord is going to send your future spouse may not be the best way to spend your time.

I have found that the countless hours I spent thinking and crying about a future spouse have only placed doubt in my heart and mind. I found myself ignoring the promises of God and even contemplating going against His plans, in order to fill the void of not having a spouse. In the times when you feel the loneliest, you should cling to Him. He knows the desires of your heart and He will give them to you, in His timing and according to His will. Sometimes, before He does that, He wants to strengthen the relationship that He has with you.

He knows the importance of having a relationship with Him before you find your spouse. If you ever lose your spouse, you will know who to cling to, during your time of loneliness. The Lord knows what we need and what we can handle, but He will never bless you without equipping you to receive the blessing. For example, He will never bless you with a car and no way to pay for it or bless you with a job without any way to get there.

I have found that the things that are from the Lord tend to come together, in ways that only He can organize. The road will not always be easy. However, when God opens doors, things will fall into place the way that He planned for them to happen. You will know that it was because of Him these things happened.

There have been times in my life when I thought things were from the Lord but they brought constant struggle and ended in disaster. The things that were from the Lord always fell into place, and I always find myself thanking the Lord for the previously closed door.

Think about a time when the Lord has opened a door for you. How did you know that it was from Him? I believe that the Lord is not the author of confusion and disorder. His adversary has already filled that position. When things are from the Lord, you will have peace about what has been given to you, even if you are faced with obstacles. This same rule applies to your love life. If God intends for you to be married, trust that it will happen despite what things may look like.

When you start to feel anxious because you don't understand how something will happen, remember Proverbs 3:5-6, *Trust in the LORD with all your heart and lean not on your own understanding; in all your ways submit to him, and he will make your paths straight (NIV)*.

Society places so many expectations on how we should live and the timelines we should follow. It makes it very difficult to simply sit in the present. However, Jesus spoke about taking it one day at a time in Matthew 6:34, He said, *so don't worry about tomorrow, for tomorrow will bring its own worries. Today's trouble is enough for today (NLT).* He highlights that the problems of today are already so much that we mustn't fret about the things of tomorrow. Jesus knew, over 2000 years ago, the daily troubles that we would face and provided us with instructions to focus on troubles one day a time. If you haven't taken care of what needs to be done today, how can you truly worry about tomorrow?

The concept of taking it one day at a time reminds me of the strategy used to stay sober, by those in Alcoholics Anonymous. For some people, the thought of staying sober for the rest of their lives can be overwhelming. Many people decide to take the approach of just thinking about getting through the next 24 hours, without taking a drink. The next day, they keep the same focus on getting to the next day and so on. I believe that when you are single, waiting on a spouse, this same approach can be applied.

When you find yourself overwhelmed by the unknown amount of time you have to wait, before you meet your future spouse, tell yourself that you can surely make it through the next 24 hours. Keep telling yourself this, until you are comfortable in your single season. This will by no means, speed up the process you must go through, to meet your spouse because only God knows when you will be ready. However, it will help you make it through the days when you feel like you cannot spend another moment being single.

Praying daily is also an excellent way to help you take it one day at a time. You can spend your time focusing on the things of that day and take them to the Lord. When you find yourself longing for a spouse or feeling lonely, talk to Jesus. He is always there for us when we need Him. He is just waiting for us to talk to him. I also believe that this practice will help you in the future when you do get married. You will feel more comfortable communicating your feelings with someone else because you have spent your time alone speaking with Christ.

Getting quiet before the Lord is also a way for Him to work on your heart and fill it with His goodness and love. There is no greater feeling than the presence of the Holy Spirit, especially during times of loneliness. It may seem hard to believe, but in the times where you may feel the most alone, you can feel the warmth of the Spirit around you. Jesus describes the Holy Spirit as the Comforter (John 14:16, KJV), and this is true. The Holy Spirit comforts us during our toughest moments. Your time of singleness is a time where you will become very familiar with the comfort that the Holy Spirit provides, during your times of doubt and loneliness.

Your emotions will change drastically, as your days come and go. There will be times when you feel completely satisfied with being single, and there will be other times when you feel completely miserable as you wait on the Lord. I describe the feeling as miserable because there are times when you may feel like you are suffocating or simply just want to give up on the thought of love because it feels that it may never happen. These times of doubt are when you need to cling to the promises of Jesus the most, even when you don't want to do so.

The enemy works to steal, destroy, and kill us. The enemy will fill your heart with doubt and anxiety that will simply tear you apart and cause you to seriously question your faith. When you start to feel this way, take a deep breath and reflect on the promises of the Lord.

There are so many people in the Bible who had to take it one day at a time, while they awaited the promises of the Lord.

Noah spent 120 years building the Ark, without one day of rain (Genesis 6:3-7, ESV). You can imagine what he was feeling, as he spent that time waiting for the Lord to fulfill His promise. I'm sure there may have been some instances of doubt, especially when he was ridiculed for obeying the Lord. Those of us who are waiting on our spouse can relate to this. I am sure you have had the opportunity to be with someone who probably didn't look like anything the Lord promised. So, you passed them over.

There may be some people who label you as "silly or crazy" because all they see is that your lonely and how you should be thankful to just have someone. What I have learned is that everyone will not always understand the things that the Lord has promised, and they are not meant to. You will have to learn how to stand confidently on the promises of the Lord. As long as you know what He has for you, you will be able to continue to take it one day at a time, as you wait on His promises.

This makes me think of Jacob. I'm sure many people in the Bible thought it was crazy when Jacob worked 14 years just to marry

Rachel (Genesis 29 NIV). He could've easily given up, accepting Leah after the first seven years of working for her father, but he knew what he had been promised. His obedience helped save his family in the long run, because Rachel gave birth to Joseph, and Joseph saved the Israelites during the plague (Genesis 46 ESV).

This story is a prime example of what the enemy meant for bad, the Lord meant for good. If we just keep focused on the Lord and His promises, He will supply us with all that we need. I am sure Jacob had to focus on taking it one day at a time, as he worked those extra seven years to be with Rachel. I admire his loyalty and faithfulness to what he knew the Lord had for him.

We live in a society of instant gratification. Everything we can think of is simply a click away, which makes waiting on the Lord very difficult. Despite what society says, please keep in mind that the promises of the Lord are real and He performs miracles each and every day. When this single life gets overwhelming, take a deep breath, and take it one day a time.

PERSONAL CHALLENGE

1. Write your thoughts and prayers in a journal for 30 days
2. Try deep breathing and meditation for 30 days
3. Spend 30 days writing 1 thing you are grateful for on a posted note and place it somewhere you can see it.

INTROSPECTION

_____

_____

_____

_____

_____

_____

_____

_____

_____

#SINGLE SEASON: DISCOVER HOW TO BE YOUR BEST YOU'RE WHILE SINGLE

TAKE ONE DAY A TIME

USE YOUR TIME WISELY

Time management is something that is very important to me. I tend to be a stickler for time. I'm obsessed with being on time and making the most of every minute that I have. Ever since I was a teenager, I was not a fan of wasting time. There were times when we would go to hang out and for about thirty minutes, we would just stand around not doing anything. This would drive me crazy because I felt like we could be using the time that we had together more wisely. This is exactly how I feel as a single person.

I often fill my calendar up with a million things every week. I used to sit and watch hours of television. Now, I feel compelled to spend that time advancing my life. I believe a time will come when I will be a mother and a wife who spends her free time with family. Until then, I need to accomplish the things that I may not be able to do when that time comes. This is not to say that I do not take any time to relax. I do find that I am taking advantage of each opportunity that is afforded to me, opportunities that align with God's purpose for my life.

There are many people who hesitate to take certain steps in their lives because they are waiting until they get married. The problem with this thinking is that it causes you to pass on opportunities that could actually lead you to the one that God has for you. For example, you may not want to travel the world because you are waiting until God sends your spouse to you. Consider this, what if you are meant to meet your spouse on that trip that you have been holding out on taking? We never know what is just around the corner for us. However, the God that we serve is all-knowing and all-seeing.

We must trust Him and not limit ourselves because we may just be delaying our time in discovering our purpose, and possibly the one that God has for us. Has this ever happened to you? Have you ever been praying to God for something, but it requires some action from you? You spend nights crying or complaining to God about how He has not answered your prayer; however, you also haven't done your part. During these times you may find that, as soon as you take your step, God answers your prayer with ease. You then realize that you were the cause of your delay. You procrastinated when it came to doing your part.

I can honestly say that I am very guilty of doing this. There are so many nights that I cried to the Lord begging Him to answer my prayer, knowing that there was some action required on my part, but I was too afraid to do it. Fear and doubt can cause you to suffer much longer than you need to. During the times that you are praying to God to do a great work in your life, you must be willing to trust Him and be willing to act in faith, even when you are unsure. This is addressed, in James Chapter 2:14-16:

> *"What good is it, my brothers and sisters, if someone claims to have faith but has no deeds? Can such faith save them? 15 Suppose a brother or a sister is without clothes and daily food. 16 If one of you says to them, "Go in peace; keep warm and well fed," but does nothing about their physical needs, what good is it? 17 In the same way, faith by itself, if it is not accompanied by action, is dead" (NIV).*

James points out that even if you claim to have strong faith, you must be willing to show this in your actions. This also can be related to the phrase "actions speak louder than words". Saying you have faith in

God and showing that you have faith in God are two separate things. If you are believing that God will send you a spouse, consider this, are your actions showing this as well? You cannot pray to God to send you someone but never leave your house or put yourself in situations where you are able to meet that person.

Are you putting off doing something in your life while you wait for your spouse? If so, pray to God for discernment and start obeying His commands. If you have been wanting to take a mission trip, but are waiting for your husband or wife and God hasn't told you to wait, pack your bags and go! Do you want to buy a home? Go speak with a lender! Are you waiting to travel somewhere? Go! Is it your dream to own your own business? Start now! Do not waste valuable time, being single. This is time that you'll never get back, once married.

As I previously mentioned, I try to make the most of my time. I volunteer, travel, started two businesses, and explore new opportunities to enhance my life daily. I look at my friends, who are married with children, and their lives are rather different from mine. They have to work much harder, to balance their time between their families and doing things that they want to do. I never want to be in a situation where I regret my family. So, I utilize the time that I have now to make more time for them later. This is not to say that my friends regret their families; however, I know how I am. I know that I would have regrets if I were not able to accomplish certain things in my life, prior to having a family of my own.

The most important way that I use my time is by building my relationship with God. I believe that if two individuals are spending their time working on themselves and growing with God when they do find each other, their bond will be that much stronger. I admit that there are many days that I get frustrated with waiting because it feels like I've been in this season for too long. Never the less, I know that the God we serve is always on time and He is preparing me for the next season in my life. Despite my impatience, I prefer to wait for God's timing, rather than my own.

I know that all things work together for the good of those who love God according to his purpose (Romans 8:28). As you are thinking about how you spend your time, ask yourself: Are you prepared to receive the spouse that you prepared for? Are you ready to be the spouse that someone else has prayed for? If you can't answer yes, to both of these questions, then you know why you may be waiting a little longer than others around you. Are you spending your time as a single person doing things that will prepare you to not only be a spouse, but to thrive in a marriage? If you can't answer yes to this question, then you could benefit from using your time more wisely.

If you answered "no" to any of the above questions, what is the next step you need to take to turn that "no" into a "yes"? Do you need therapy? Do you need to get your finances in order? Do you have goals that you still need to accomplish? Use this time to address these areas now.

I don't know about you, but I have been praying for a spouse for so long that when that day comes, I don't want to waste any time on things that I could have been working on, during my single season. I want to be spending that time investing in my marriage and my kids.

Think about how much easier it is to go to school or start a business when you only have yourself to worry about it. My married friends are always telling me not to rush and that I should enjoy my singleness. I now share that same advice with you. Use your time wisely, during this season, and you will be able to make the most of your next season.

SELF-REFLECTION:

1. Are you spending your time wisely?
2. Do you meet the requirements on your own list for a future spouse?
3. What areas of your life do you need to work on?
4. What can you do now as a single person that would be more difficult to do as a spouse and/or parent?
5. What is holding you back?
6. What have been you putting off doing?

INTROSPECTION

1. No
2. Some but not all.
3. Finances, Being more dependent on God. Work in Faith and Finishing school. Paying off Debt.
4. Going to School, Spend more time with God and Walk by faith wherever He leads me.

5. Me myself and I
6. School/studying and saving.

USE YOUR TIME WISELY

ENJOY SPENDING TIME ALONE

Over the course of my adult life, I have spent quite a bit of time alone. There are so many days I ask God, "How long must I endure this time alone?" There are some days that I believe that He answers me with a simple "Hold On!", and other days, I am answered in a deafening silence. It is like when you ask your parents the same question one million-plus times and they stop answering because they know they have already answered the first five hundred thousand times. Even though we know the answer, we keep asking as though we are hoping that, by asking, things will happen sooner.

Everything happens according to God's perfect timing, and I sincerely believe there will be a time when I will be praying to God to have an opportunity to spend time alone. During my times of loneliness, I simply stop to thank God for the blessings He has already given me. Even when I don't want to spend so much time alone, I know that there is a reason for everything, and we just have to be thankful to God for, where He has us at that moment.

This brings me back to a time when I was unemployed for two months. Because I was so used to working and having a certain level of comfort, it was the longest 2 months of my life. I spent every single day, of those two months, searching for a job and worrying about what would happen, when my savings ran out. The entire time that I spent worrying, the Holy Spirit was telling me to just relax and enjoy the time off, because I would need it.

Of course, I just shrugged it off and kept worrying about what I would do when I no longer had savings. As God would have it, I was down to my last $300 but, at the same time, I started my new job, and never found out what happened when my savings ran out.

The funny thing is that I worked so much on my new job that I would work two weeks at a time without one day off. About one month into working two weeks straight, I had to laugh at my impatience and distrust because God was giving me a much-needed vacation that I could not enjoy because I had to be in control.

Fast forward eight years later. I wished that I could have two months off. I use this example to show that we should embrace our circumstances, even when we don't understand, because God does understand. He does nothing without a purpose.

As we often hear, He is all-knowing and all-seeing. In this situation, God knew that I would need time off and that I would be overworked and extremely tired when my new job started. He was giving me a much-needed vacation, to prepare m for what was in store.

This takes me back to the book of Genesis, when God gave Joseph the dream of the skinny cows eating the fat cows. This was a foreshadowing for Pharaoh to store up as much food as possible, during the seven years of abundance, to account for the seven years of famine (Genesis 41 NIV). During my time of unemployment, I was so focused on my discomfort, I overlooked what God was trying to tell me.

During my times of singleness, I often had to think back to this time and how I wish I would have trusted God and had taken the time to enjoy that much needed time off. I would give anything to be able to take two months off, just to relax and enjoy this life that God has given me. I think about what I could have been doing versus what I did do, and I truly wish I could go back in time and relive that time all over again, doing it differently.

When I complain about being single and having so much alone time, I think 5 years from now, I could be wishing and hoping for one stolen moment to myself. I imagine that if God answers my prayer for a husband and two children, there won't be many moments to be alone. I see parents complain, often, about not being able to go to the bathroom, without having their toddler tagging along. I cannot even imagine what that would be like. I advise you to just simply say, "thank you", when you find yourself complaining about spending time alone, because you may not get that future opportunity that God has for you.

Now think back to some key times that you spent alone and were not happy, about those times. How did you spend that time? One moment that really stands out to me, is when I found myself alone on an Easter Sunday. I remember going to church and being excited to celebrate my Lord and Savior, only to find myself feeling sad and alone. Seeing many families together, smiling and taking pictures, really made me feel like I was missing out on something. During a time that I should have been excited to celebrate a grand occasion, the enemy was winning as he filled my mind with the constant reminder that I had no family of my own.

I had planned to go out to eat with my friends, who are married, and then they invited another married couple, and I immediately felt sad because I did not want to be the fifth wheel. I decided that I wouldn't go and I left church feeling so broken and upset, on a day of joy and celebration.

Feeling defeated, I went home, laid in bed and cried. I took a quick nap, trying to sleep away my reality. Napping had become one of the ways that I coped with my single life. When I was sleeping, I could have any life that I wanted. Waking up and facing the truth is what was hard for me. I now know that I could have handled the situation in so many other ways, but during that moment, what I was doing felt right.

What I should have done was spend some time doing something that I enjoyed or trying something new. I could've also taken that moment to be thankful for the sacrifice that the Lord made, and just simply be alone with Him, in His presence. If God brought my husband today, I most likely wouldn't get that moment to be alone with Him, on Resurrection Sunday. I can only imagine how things will change when I am married.

When you put things into perspective in this way, it makes spending time alone more worth it. Just think, if you had to spend a year spending all of your time alone in order to spend the next 50 years with a spouse and children, how would that make you feel? As a person who values my alone time, I am more apt to enjoy being alone when I remind myself that this time alone may only be temporary. I have grown to truly value this time of solitude as I think about the many years I could have filled with my family.

I'm sure you have asked the question, "When will this season be over?" I ask you, "Does it really matter?" Whether it's one year or ten years, do those single years spending time alone, compared to the many years that you could spend with your future family? As a single person, this makes me hopeful and excited that God loves me so much that He is giving me the alone time that He knows I need. He is allowing me to enjoy moments that I may not be able to enjoy as when I'm a wife and a mother.

As I continue to write this chapter, I realize that I may not have been able to write this book had I not been single. It has taken me long enough to write it while trying to juggle a full-time job, two small businesses, and the demands of my personal life. If I added wife and mother to the list, it would be next to impossible to complete this book.

Writing a book has been something that God placed on my heart, ever since I was thirteen years old, and I know that He intends for me to accomplish what He placed in my heart. This simple revelation makes me value the time that I have, as a single person, even more. I know that I have a God that loves me so much that He is giving me the time that I need to accomplish the goals that I set, as a young child.

I imagine that if I had gotten married at 25, the way that I had planned it, my life would be very different. I probably wouldn't have my Master's degree. I most likely would not have gone on my mission trip to Belize, visited Dubai, started my two businesses, nor would I have had the time to spend volunteering, which in turn helped me to land my dream job.

I also would not be able to dedicate time to my job or accomplish the things that I need to. My job allows me to travel all over the country, which is something that I prayed for. If I had gotten married when I wanted to, I probably would have had a child under the age of 2 by now. Therefore, I wouldn't be open to traveling all over the country, for work.

These are experiences that I am grateful for. Had I gotten married when I wanted to, I may have not had the opportunities I've had or the value of the experiences would be so different. The things that I have experienced in my life and will experience in my single life, are worth the unwanted time alone. Think about where you are right now, in your life. Look at the things you have accomplished and would like to accomplish. Now ask yourself this question: Would I have been able to do this without spending time alone?

PERSONAL CHALLENGE:

1. Go do something that you have been waiting to do with someone else, alone.
2. Make doing things alone a regular activity.
3. Enjoy a holiday alone.
4. Create a life that you don't have to regularly escape from.

INTROSPECTION

ENJOY SPENDING TIME ALONE

#SINGLE SEASON: DISCOVER HOW TO BE YOUR BEST YOU'RE WHILE SINGLE

BE VIGILANT WHEN DATING

When you are single, there will be people who come along who will excite you in ways that you could never imagine, but you must be careful not to let this excitement get in the way of where you are with God. Make sure that this person is sent from the Lord, and that they won't distract you from what God has called you to be.

Sometimes we yearn for someone so much that when someone comes along, we don't stop to consult with God to make sure that they have been given permission to be in our lives. We are just so excited that someone has finally noticed us that we jump in head first, without discerning whether this is a trick of the enemy. Is this who God called you to be with or is this simply a counterfeit?

Now, let's think about counterfeits. When you see those counterfeit purses at the flea market, they look like the real thing. I'm sure many of us have purchased at least one in our lives. The thing about a counterfeit is that you can always tell it is not the real thing, upon close examination or putting it next to the real thing. If you have a counterfeit item, closely inspect it. I guarantee you will find a flaw. It could be something small, like the label or the wrong color thread used. It easily passes for the real thing until you look closer.

The enemy will send someone into your life who looks like everything you asked for. You look at the list (we all have one in some shape or form) and this person meets all the requirements. They treat you well, give you all the attention you could ever ask for, and they look good on paper. "Lord, this must be the one!" We get so caught up on what these people are presenting on the outside that we forget to inspect and examine them on the inside.

As you spend more time with these individuals, you must examine whether their actions align with their words. Do they say they love Jesus, but tempt you to succumb to your convictions? Do they say they have a relationship with Jesus, but you don't see evidence of said relationship? You must use discernment in these situations. We know that God works in mysterious ways and He just may send you someone that needs a little more polishing and growth spiritually, and this is fine. But if that person is causing you to stumble, remember that the Lord's blessings do not cause you to sin.

Be mindful of who you allow into your life romantically. This is not to say that they are bad people, they could be completely wonderful. It could just mean that they are not who God meant for you. Marriage is so much more than finding someone to spend the rest of your life with. It is about finding the one that you can grow spiritually with and who will draw you closer to God, not pull you away. I believe a godly spouse will catapult you into your destiny and push you closer to your purpose. These marriages aren't easy, but they are God-filled and divine. Marriage with the one that God has designed for you is worth waiting for, despite how hard it may be to wait on it.

My advice to you would be to pray to God and ask Him to block anything that He did not send to you before you become invested in the relationship. Praying this prayer, after you have developed feelings, will certainly make it that much harder to obey God's word and it could be devastating for you. I have had this happen to me.

Someone from my past came back into my life. He was someone that I always thought about. I truly thought that he was the one that got away. We reconnected and entered a whirlwind relationship. It was AMAZING, but it also scared me because I never once stopped to consult with God about him.

I prayed to God to block this relationship if it was not in His will for me. I tried to avoid this prayer for a few weeks because I already knew what God was going to say, and I wasn't ready to let this marvelous relationship go. Never the less, God blocked the relationship and it went from bliss to pure heartbreak. I hadn't hurt like this in a long time. It felt like someone had ripped my heart out and stabbed me a million times.

Despite my devastation, all I could do was repent and cling to God. I couldn't bring myself to be mad that He took such a wonderful relationship from me, because I knew that He was only protecting me from what I could not see. Sometimes people come into our lives and we believe they must be from God because we have been waiting for so long for someone to notice us. So, when someone does, we immediately think that the person was sent from God.

When you find yourself in these situations, you must immediately go to God about the person, as soon as they come into your life. Do not make the mistake that I did: waiting until it was too late to ask God if he was sent from Him. Looking back, I know that I should have prayed about the situation before we even spoke to each other. Now I wonder if God ever meant for me to reach out to him. Was it simply my loneliness leading me down the wrong path?

When you have been called to serve the Lord, the enemy is constantly trying to destroy and kill you whether it be emotionally, mentally, physically or spiritually. You must guard your heart, as it says in Proverbs 4:23 – *Above all else guard your heart for everything you do flows from it* – *what better way for the enemy to destroy you than for him to attack the thing where everything flows (NIV).*

Have you ever tried to serve God with a broken heart? It can be very hard. Despite my heartache, I clung to God for dear life because I knew that He was the only person that could put the pieces of my heart back together. This was not always my response, and generally is not the response of most people, especially when you have been praying to God to send you someone. I used to find myself mad at God and I would completely stop talking to Him; however, I found that during this time, I was only hurting myself. Through maturity and developing a relationship with God, I learned to cling to Him always, but especially in my darkest hours.

The hardest thing that I dealt with, during this time, was knowing that I broke my 16 months of celibacy and my promise to God to remain celibate until marriage. Despite losing a person who I truly believed was my soulmate, I struggled most with disappointing God. It would have been easy for me to hide from Him, out of guilt and shame, but I knew better and I latched on to Him and refused to let Him go.

The enemy only wanted to use my guilt and shame to isolate me, but I would not allow him to win. I did not make a clean break with the person that I broke up with and this heartache dragged on for a few months. I spent many sleepless nights and days dealing with anxiety, hoping that the relationship would be restored. One night, before I went to bed, I begged God to restore the relationship. In the middle of the night, I heard God speak to me. He said, "I can restore the relationship now or you can wait and receive all that I have for you".

I must admit, I was startled because I was not expecting to hear His voice so clearly. I chose to wait for what God had for me, but that still didn't mean I did not try to hang on to the relationship for a while. However, God made sure that the relationship would not be restored because the individual made it clear that, despite how I felt for him, he did share the same feelings. Even though he always remained nice, his actions made it clear that he was no longer interested in being with me. This realization hurt me a lot.

I spent many nights crying and struggling to deal with the realization that I broke my celibacy and promise to God, for a counterfeit relationship. I admit that the enemy almost won this battle because I almost gave up on fighting. Thankfully, I chose to take the experience, learn from it and include it in this book. Had I never had this heartbreak; I wouldn't be able to share my lesson with you. I am learning to see the blessing in the lesson instead of dwelling on the pain.

The lessons that I learned from this experience are:

1. **Pray to God as soon as a new person comes into your life.** Continue to pray to God about the person and do not hesitate to ask God to block what He did not send. You won't believe how fast He will block

what intends to harm you.

2. **Closely examine them through discernment and God's word;** If you are praying for a godly man or woman and the person in your life doesn't even have a prayer life, it is likely this person is not from God.

3. **When you realize that someone is not from God, LET THEM GO**! Do not try to hold on to what God never meant for you to have. You are only preventing yourself from receiving who God truly does have for you;

4. **Remember that God is in control** and trust that He has a plan for your life.

Sometimes it can become hard to wait on God, but it is better to be single and satisfied than to be married to someone that God never intended you to be with. It may be tempting to take things in your own hands and try to force a relationship, but I encourage you to always think back to Abraham and Sarah. Instead of waiting for God to send the son they prayed for, they chose to take things in their own hands. I encourage you to wait for Isaac and not to create an Ishmael (Genesis 16 ESV).

SELF-REFLECTION:

1. Have you prayed to God about the person that you are dating?
2. Does the person you are dating treat you the way that you want to be treated?
3. Is the person you are dating actions align with who they say they are?
4. Is the person you are dating in alignment with your purpose in life?
5. Does the person that you are dating bring value to your life?
6. Does the person tempt you to succumb to your convictions?

INTROSPECTION

Be vigilant when dating

Be vigilant when dating

Don't Settle: Who You Want versus Who You Need

This chapter is closely related to the previous one. However, this will focus on who you want versus who you need. As a single person, there will come a time when you will have to evaluate what you want versus what you need, in a future spouse. You may be looking for a person that fits your list of ideals, but God wants to bless you with someone who looks nothing like what you think you want. We think we know who we want, but God already knows who we need. The question is, will you be obedient to God and refuse to settle for less than His best for you?

This is not to say that the person that you are with is not a good person. He or she could be an amazing and godly individual, but that doesn't mean they are for you. As we are waiting for our future spouses, we must consistently pray to God for His will to be done and not our own. Often, we have a vision of what we think our lives should look like, and it does not always align with God's will for our lives. We truly must be willing to trust God to provide us with what He knows we need and not what we think we want.

If you are reading this book and you are currently in a relationship or considering one, I encourage you to closely examine the relationship to ensure it satisfies what you need. For example, if you are in a relationship with someone who treats you like a king or queen, respects you, loves you, and the relationship is everything you ever wanted but, the person does not draw you closer to God. Do you think that this is a relationship that you need?

We know that everything that we do should honor the Lord, so if your relationship is not pushing you towards Him, it is time to evaluate whose will is being done. It would also be important to establish a list of what you want versus what you need so that you are aligned with God's will for your life. Are you in a relationship that is headed towards marriage, or are you simply just "seeing where things go"?

You know God would not want you to be in a relationship that will not lead to marriage. Once again, it is better to be single than to be with someone that God never intended you to be in a relationship with.

When you spend time with who you want and not who God knows you need, you delay living God's preferred future for your life. I know that it can be hard to let go of a relationship that you believe is perfect, but you do not want to settle for what is not God's best. I believe that there are people living great lives, but they are not living the best life that God has for them, because they were not obedient to God's will. I do not know about you, but I always want the best of what God has for me. I never want to spend a day of my life questioning whether I am living the best life that God planned for me.

I know that being single can be hard, and even lonely at times. I have cried many nights and even prayed for God to remove my desire for a husband because I was growing weary of waiting. I have prayed this prayer for many years and yet, God still has not removed the desire. After my last relationship, I know that I am meant to be married, but I must be patient and wait for God's best.

Many times, we think what we want is best for us, but we truly are wrong. Let's think back to Sarah. She thought she had her life all figured out and that if Hagar bore a child, they would all live happily ever after. She could not have been more wrong. This is the first sign that Ishmael was not what God intended because Sarah had to manipulate the situation to get the blessing, she believed she wanted (Genesis 16 & 17, ESV).

When God wants you to have something, there isn't anything or anyone that will prevent you from receiving it. God will instruct you with what you need to do and, until you hear from Him, your best bet is to be still or you will find yourself feeling like Sarah (Genesis 16 & 17 ESV) Sarah's disobedience didn't just affect her, but three other people were affected by the choice that she made.

The same is for you, when you are disobedient to God and remain in a relationship that you want, but not the one you need to be in. Your actions are affecting three other people: your current partner, their future spouse, and your future spouse. While you two remain in a relationship that is not in God's will, you block four people from living the best life that God has for them.

Do you want to wake up ten years from now and question whether you are living the best life that God has or you? This is when you must have a hard conversation with yourself and be willing to end what God is saying "no" to and be prepared to say "yes" to what He knows is His best for you.

Another way to determine if you are in the relationship that you want or in the one that you need is to examine how the relationship aligns with your purpose. If God is calling you into ministry and your future spouse doesn't want anything to do with ministry, let alone go to church, do you think that this is the best relationship for you? If you know that God is calling you to be a missionary and your future spouse doesn't want to leave the country, do you believe that God wants you to be in a marriage where you will be serving Him alone? Is this relationship pleasing you or the Lord?

Ultimately, we must die to ourselves and pursue the things that God wants for us. Marriage is not just for our satisfaction; it is meant to be pleasing to the Lord. If your relationship is not pleasing to the Lord, then you already know what you must do. You first need to refer to the last chapter and ask God was the person sent by Him and then you need to look at what you want versus what God knows you need and be willing to sacrifice the relationship to receive the best that God has for you.

When God spoke to me in the middle of the night, telling me that He indeed would restore the relationship that I was praying for or I could wait for all that He had for me, there was no question of what I would do. I do admit, there are times where I wish that I could have my cake and eat it too, meaning that I get to keep the relationship I wanted until God gave me what I needed. However, I know that God does not work this way. He wasn't going to send any of His children into a messy situation, so I knew that choosing His best meant that I had to let go of what I wanted.

Though it was painful, I do not regret the decision I made that night because I know that, if I thought a particular relationship was amazing, then what God has for me is greater than anything that I could ever imagine. I am embracing the season that God has me in, despite its challenges at times. This is because I know that He knows exactly what I need. I have also been able to gain a better understanding of what I need in a life partner.

I once believed that a good resume indicated a suitable mate. I was proven to be wrong. For me, it isn't enough to be financially stable, educated, and have a good career. I need someone who is going to pour into me spiritually and be mentally and emotionally stable. I need someone who is healed and has done the self-work required to be able to give themselves fully to someone else. As you contemplate your relationship or potential relationship, think about your needs and not necessarily what you may want.

PERSONAL CHALLENGE:

1. Create a list and write down what you want on one side and write down what you need on the other side.
2. Pray over your list and ask God for discernment, courage, and wisdom.
3. If you are dating someone, identify if they have the qualities on your needs list. What will you do if they don't meet your needs?

INTROSPECTION

_____

_____

_____

_____

_____

_____

DON'T SETTLE: WHO YOU WANT VERSUS WHO YOU NEED

#SINGLE SEASON: DISCOVER HOW TO BE YOUR BEST YOU'RE WHILE SINGLE

STAY READY AND YOU WON'T HAVE TO GET READY

As you are living your single life and making the most of the time that you have, you must also be getting ready to receive the relationship that God has for you, if it is in His will. If you are praying for God to send you a godly spouse, you must ask yourself, are you the godly spouse that your potential spouse has been praying for? We can't expect God to send us something that we are not.

What are you doing to get ready for your spouse? What strongholds must be broken? What does your prayer life look like? Are you the spouse that you are praying for? If you answered "no" to any of these questions, then you need to start preparing to be what you are asking for. God's timing is perfect, but we also must be prepared. Ecclesiastes 3:1 says, "There is a time for everything and a season for every activity under the heavens (NIV). Have you ever thought that maybe you aren't waiting on God to send you a spouse, but God is waiting on you to send you a spouse? What habits do you need to break? We have already identified that God wants the best for His children. Are you the best for His son or daughter? If you can't honestly answer "yes" to this question, then it's time for you to start getting prepared. One of my favorite sayings is "if you stay ready, you never have to get ready".

You should be working on yourself and your foundation as a single individual as you wait to receive your helpmeet. Marriage exposes your flaws and the shortcomings that you have as a single person. So many people think that marriage is the answer. You must identify your flaws and shortcomings before the marriage and address these issues before you become one with someone else.

Another thing to consider is whether you are whole as a single person. If you are waiting for your "other half" and you believe you are incomplete without your spouse, this is something that you need to address immediately. We MUST first be completely whole by ourselves before we can become one with someone else. Society has taught us that we don't become whole until we are married, but this is so untrue. As I have illustrated throughout this book, it is important to develop your life as a single person before you consider life with someone else. You must know and understand who you are before you can know and understand someone else.

Nothing is promised to us, so if you go through life believing that your "other half" is somewhere on this earth waiting to complete you, you may never come into everything that God has for you because you will have wasted time waiting for someone to complete you. You also must consider that a spouse is not guaranteed. What if you have waited all this time for your spouse and Jesus comes back before you get married? Will you be satisfied with the life that you led, and will Jesus be pleased?

If the Lord sent your spouse to you today, would you be ready to receive what He has for you? I need you to think very hard about this. Are you truly ready to be married? Could you spend more time savoring the single life as you prepare for the Lord to send your future spouse? Work on becoming content in the season that you are currently in. If you are unable to be with yourself, then how do you expect someone to want to be with you?

There are two key areas that are very important that people tend to overlook, while they are single, but tend to cause issues in a relationship. One of these areas is financial stability and the other area is mental health.

I will explain why each of these areas is important and MUST be addressed prior to bringing someone else into your life. My last relationship did not work because these two areas were not addressed during my ex-partner's single season.

When I met him, I admit, I was a little hesitant because he didn't look like what I was used to. After our first date, I was totally intrigued. One day he told me that he wanted to be exclusive, very shortly after our first date. I remember being caught off guard, but excited. I then thought back to somethings about his past that he shared with me and wondered if he was completely healed. However, he presented himself as a devout Christian man, and he fit every attribute in my prayer journal. "This surely had to be the one, right?"

While washing dishes one day I totally thought I heard God say, "he might not be what you want, but he is who you need". I remember thinking to myself, "seriously?" Then I said, "okay God, I trust you". We went out that night and next thing you know we were officially in a relationship. When I say things flipped immediately, they flipped like a quarter in a coin toss. He went from being so sweet and holy, to discussing an encounter with an ex-girlfriend which ended with him saying, "f-you" about the lady. This utterance totally caught me off guard, but I just diverted the conversation and changed the subject. Looking back, I realize that this was a sign of a person with some unresolved issues in his past that were affecting his mental and emotional health.

Despite trying to conceal them, it became evident that the deeply traumatic abuse from his past that had gone unresolved prevented his ability to truly trust people and to be transparent with anyone. This made the relationship challenging because the simplest of disagreements turned into dramatic exchanges that were totally uncalled for. It was early in the relationship that I realized that I had made a mistake and it became more and more evident why there was such a rush to get into a relationship.

This same individual had not reached a level of financial stability that he was comfortable with. This caused me to feel uneasy anytime that I wanted to do something that required spending money, because I knew that he would bring up how he was trying to save money and he had goals that he wanted to achieve. This became a source of frustration for me because I was much younger and had been working very hard to become financially stable. I began to resent him for not working on this goal before he brought me into his life.

Nevertheless, the relationship didn't work out, for many reasons, including me feeling like I was not supported emotionally when I was going through a very rough time in my life. He also used his financial instability and need to focus on his goals as a reason not to continue the relationship. I was devastated because the break up came at a tough time in my life, but I also was grateful because God was saving me from what I couldn't see. I later found out that he had unresolved issues with an ex-girlfriend and had chosen to work on things with her.

I remember asking him why he had pushed for a relationship, knowing he wasn't ready. His response was "I suck sometimes". It was at that moment, I realized that people get into relationships thinking that they are ready, and often conclude that they aren't ready after the damage has been done. Even though I know, at times, we want to be in a relationship, sometimes it isn't what we need.

Sometimes we must be disciplined and do what we don't want to do in order to get to where we want to be.

This relationship was also a wake-up call for me. I had to do some serious self-reflection to understand how I ended up in this situation. I realized that I still had my own work to do, and there were some issues that were unresolved from my past that I needed to address before I could truly be with someone else.

I began to understand how my own personal traumas affected the ways that I connected with others and that I needed to work on those areas in my life. I also had to reevaluate my relationship with God and ask for His forgiveness, guidance, love, and comfort as I began my journey of healing.

I especially had to examine my relationship with God because I had to understand how I misunderstood what I heard that day I was washing dishes. I needed to spend more time reconnecting with Him and discerning His voice. It was during this time of deep reflection that I realized that Jesus was enough for me.

What does your relationship with God look like? Is He enough? If He isn't enough, then no one will ever truly be enough. This is the time to work on you and your relationship with God. I can tell you from personal experience that the loneliness you may be feeling does not change when you get in a relationship. You must become whole and content with yourself well before He sends someone into your life.

It is not until you understand the love that you receive from God that you truly understand what it means to give and receive love. What better way to learn how to love than to spend your single learning how to love and receive love from God? One of the greatest benefits of being single is learning to love yourself. When you learn to love yourself, what you accept changes. Self-love will also drive you to be better and live better. It is only then that you will be ready.

SELF-REFLECTION:

1. Who are you?
2. What do you need to work on to get prepared for the next season?
3. What does your relationship with God look like? How can you make this relationship better?
4. Are your finances in order? Do you have a financial advisor?
5. Is there anything or anyone from your past that is holding you back?

INTROSPECTION

STAY READY AND YOU WON'T HAVE TO GET READY

#SINGLE SEASON: DISCOVER HOW TO BE YOUR BEST YOU'RE WHILE SINGLE

UNDERSTAND THAT IT WON'T ALWAYS BE EASY

One of the reasons that it has taken me so long to write this book is because I have struggled with accepting my singleness, during this season. Feelings of loneliness, disappointment, anxiety, and anger have consumed me many times during this journey, and it has made it difficult to appreciate being in this place in life. While this book is meant to empower you and encourage you to be your best, I also want it to be authentic. I would be remiss if I didn't acknowledge that being single isn't always easy, but in many cases is necessary.

Have you found yourself at a breaking point and felt like you just simply couldn't continue living this single life? I have, but I have had to remind myself many times that God has me here for a reason. As much as I know that God always does what's in my best interest, I truly struggle to accept this fact when I have my days. Those days where I lie in bed crying about how "horrible" my life is. It is during these days that I doubt the promises of God and I throw myself a pity party. Does this change anything? No, not at all, but some days I convince myself that this type of thinking makes me feel better.

I want you to know that if you have ever felt this way or are experiencing these feelings right now, you are not alone. There have been times that I have been smiling on the outside and dying on the inside because I felt I had reached my breaking point. Understand that it is ok to be in your feelings, just don't stay in them. If you need to take a day to be upset, to scream, cry, call out to the Lord, then you do what you feel that you need to do. However, do not allow this to be your go-to response.

Speaking from my own experience, if you allow yourself to stay in this place for too long, it begins to consume you and change you. Find ways to channel this energy into positive outlets. I found that exercise, especially running or kickboxing, will help to let out your emotions of anger, disappointment, hurt, pain, etc. Try writing your feelings on paper or record yourself expressing your feelings. Try finding a trusted friend to talk to and help you to identify facts that you may have overlooked.

As you continue to navigate your single journey, there will be constant reminders of your singleness along the way. It is up to you, regarding how you to respond to them. I challenge you to come up with your own list of reminders of why your singleness is necessary at this time in your life. I then want you to internalize what you have put on this list and bring these points to mind when you find yourself in your feelings.

There will also be times when you are angry at God because He isn't moving according to your timing. It is during this time that you really should get into your word and reset how you are thinking and feeling. While it is not uncommon to be angry at God, it is during this time that we may make the most unwise choices. We tend to do things out of anger thinking that we are hurting God but actually, we are only hurting ourselves. It is in these moments that being single can be it's most difficult, but it is up to us to reframe our thinking, check our feelings, and reconnect with God.

We serve a jealous God who wants no one to come before Him (Exodus 34:14). If you are putting your wants for a spouse before God, that means your entire relationship with God will be contingent upon your relationship status and your relationship will likely become an idol. You can then find yourself in a situation where God could take the relationship from you to get your attention. This, in turn, will not only devastate you but, also your future spouse.

There was a time that I allowed my negative thoughts about singleness to get the best of me. One day I was livid. I told God that I was done praying and that I was no longer talking to Him. I even stopped going to church for a few Sundays because being in church listening to the pastor speak about the Lord's promises was not what I wanted to listen to. However, because of my relationship with God, this behavior didn't last long because it had become uncharacteristic to who I am.

As I reflect on this time, I realize just how disrespectful, ungrateful, and selfish my actions were. How dare I tell my Heavenly Father that I no longer wanted to speak to Him? Not only did I no longer want to speak to Him, but I wasn't going to write this book either. I quit writing for an entire year. During that time, I thought I was being rebellious, but now I know that even in my stubbornness God's plan was still unfolding.

I needed to get to a place of hurt and pain that would allow me to be real and honest about my feelings. I had to go through that low moment to be able to write this chapter. While I am not proud of that moment at all, I am grateful because I get to let you know that you are not alone in the way that you may feel. I pray that you find encouragement during your darkest and loneliest hours and that you chase after Jesus more than ever when this single season becomes too much to bear. Despite how I treated Jesus, not one time did His love for me change. This dark time also helped me realize that I wasn't ready for the relationship that I so badly wanted. I still had work to do.

The unique thing about your single season is that you are always growing and always learning. Every time you think that you may be ready, somehow you are reminded to be grateful for this singleness. This dark time revealed to me that I shut down when I don't get my way and I say things that I don't mean when I am angry. I had a difficult time because it required me to really look at myself.

When I say that understand it won't be easy, I don't mean that in reference to waiting on a spouse. I also mean standing in your truth and doing the work to become your best you will not be easy, but it is necessary.

How often have you told someone else about what they need to fix about themselves and how they should do it? How many times have you done this to yourself? How often do you evaluate yourself and put your own self on blast? I can tell you for sure, it's much easier to call others out than oneself. To become the best version of yourself, you have to be willing to face some hard truths about yourself.

I have said several times in this book that singleness is necessary, and I stand behind that statement. Think about just how ugly it can be when you face the truth about yourself and why you may still be in this season. Do you really want to experience these feelings with a significant other? I know I do not.

I have been through some things in my life, and I have also sabotaged several relationships because I hadn't properly dealt with those things before bringing someone else into my life. Healing from the things from our pasts is key to having successful relationships. Have you done the work to heal from your past?

First, you have to decide that you are ready to do the work. Then you do a self-inventory. Start by asking yourself the following questions:

1. **Am I ready** to do the work required to become the best version of me during this single season?

2. **Am I committed** to remaining single until I have done the necessary work to become whole and healed?

3. **What do I need to heal from?** Who do I need to forgive?

4. **What does being whole and healed look like for me?**

Secondly, you must take note of your answers and then create a plan to move forward.

Thirdly, pursue some form of therapy. Honestly, we all need some form of therapy whether it is to identify some deep-rooted traumas or to learn positive coping strategies to use throughout your everyday life.

Therapy can be as normal as getting your yearly wellness exam or getting maintenance on your car. Therapy isn't always used because there is an issue, it can very well be used to ensure that when an issue arises you know how to cope with your struggles. I challenge you to complete your self- inventory, devise a plan of action, and find a therapist in your area who can help you to execute your plan.

Remember that this part of the process can be very difficult, but it truly is necessary for you to be your best you.

We live in an instant gratification society and often expect relationships to just work without us having to do the work. I believe that this is part of the reason that so many relationships and marriages fail, because we are unwilling to work on the things that are unpleasant in us. If you don't address these things now, you better believe they will surface in your relationships. So again, I say to you that despite it not being easy, healing is a vital step in your single journey.

PERSONAL CHALLENGE:

1. Schedule an appointment with a therapist
2. Do a quarterly self-inventory
3. Write your feelings in a journal and take it with you to a therapy session
4. Develop a self-care regimen

INTROSPECTION

UNDERSTAND THAT IT WON'T ALWAYS BE EASY

CELEBRATE!

As you spend time in this season of singleness, I recommend that you celebrate this time. While for some it can feel like this season is never-ending, it truly is a blessing if you allow it to be. Celebrate this time that you have been given to focus on you and enjoy the things that you may not be able to enjoy in this next season in your life.

I can say that I am one of those people who feel like this season has lasted too long, but I have done my best to relish in the moment. I have started businesses, pursued higher education, and traveled all over the world. I can now add author to the growing list. I want you to be able to have your own list that you are proud of when this season is over.

If the time for me to be a wife and mother comes, I can honestly say that I made the most of my single season and walk confidently into the next season, knowing that I have done everything that I could to become the best version of myself, while I was single. I pray that this book has encouraged you during this season and has also motivated you to become the best version of you during this time.

I pray that you realize the gift that you have been given by God and you relish in this time. I pray that when this next season comes you will think back to your single season and smile. I pray that you give this season your all and that you are present. I pray that you learn how to just BE with God, during this season and that your relationships grow in ways that you did not know that they could grow.

I pray that you achieve every goal that you set, during this time. I pray that you say "yes" to the business opportunity, to the job in the new city, to the opportunity to travel the world, to the person who isn't what you want but who God knows you need, and to anything else that will help you be a better you. I pray that you say "yes" to you, in this season.

I pray that you fall in love with yourself over and over again. I pray that you know and understand your value and your worth. I pray that, during this season, you choose you, every time. During this season, I pray that you celebrate every win and loss because sometimes the losses will set us up for an even bigger win.

I pray that you allow God to order your steps, during this season. I pray that you believe in yourself, even when no one else does, and I pray that you are always your biggest cheerleader as you navigate this journey to be your best you!

In Jesus' name, Amen!

SELF-REFLECTION

1. Have you taken the time to celebrate you?

2. What does self-love look like for you?

3. What can you do to be the best you?

INTROSPECTION

_____
_____
_____
_____
_____
_____
_____
_____
_____
_____

CELEBRATE!

CELEBRATE!

#SingleSeason: Tool Kit

SELF-CARE IDEAS

Self-care is very important. As you navigate your single season, it is important that you remember to take time out for yourself and to practice healthy coping strategies. These activities are also great ways to spend some intentional time alone.

- ☐ Write in a journal

- ☐ Go to the beach

- ☐ Take a walk in the park

- ☐ Take a nap

- ☐ Turn off your cellphone for a day

- ☐ Utilize your Do Not Disturb feature on your phone

- ☐ Deactivate social media for a week

- ☐ Take a solo trip

- ☐ Plan a spa day

- ☐ Take one day a month for yourself to do what you want including doing nothing

- ☐ Exercise

- ☐ Go out for a night of dancing

- ☐ Plan a night in with friends

- ☐ Go to a comedy show

- ☐ Say "no"

- ☐ Talk with your God

- ☐ Try meditation

- ☐ Eat healthier

- ☐ Buy something nice for yourself

- ☐ Try deep breathing

- ☐ Call and catch up with an old friend

- ☐ Take a candlelit bath with soft music

- ☐ Be selfish every once in a while

- ☐ Try something new

- ☐ Get out of your comfort zone

- ☐ Read for leisure

- ☐ Go to a movie alone

- ☐ Take yourself on a date

- ☐ Watch the sunrise

- ☐ Write positive affirmations and put them in a place where you can see them every day.

- ☐ Take a road trip to clear your mind

- ☐ Dance like no one is watching

- ☐ Enjoy your favorite dessert without guilt

- ☐ Go on a random adventure

- ☐ Try yoga

- ☐ Have a good cry

- ☐ Learn a new recipe

- ☐ Host a game night with friends

- ☐ Try a painting class

- ☐ Write a song and record it even if you can't sing

- ☐ Create a bucket list

- ☐ Be intentional about who you spend your time with

- ☐ Sit in silence

- ☐ Pray

SCRIPTURES FOR TIMES OF NEED

As we know being single can be very tough. We experience so many different emotions during this season and it is very important to make sure that we are growing in our relationship with God. I hope that these scriptures will give you comfort when you find yourself struggling with being single. Write a short prayer for each emotion. You can say these prayers when you have rough times.

AT THE RIGHT TIME, I, THE LORD, WILL MAKE IT HAPPEN.

-ISAIAH 60:22 (NLT)

ANXIETY

- Psalms 55:22 Cast your cares on the LORD and he will sustain you; he will never let the righteous be shaken.
- Romans 15:13 May the God of hope fill you with all joy and peace as you trust in him, so that you may overflow with hope by the power of the Holy Spirit.
- 1 Peter 5:7 Cast all your anxiety on Him because He cares for you.
- Philippians 4:6-7 Do not be anxious about anything, but in every situation, by prayer and petition, with thanksgiving, present your requests to God. And the peace of God, which transcends all understanding, will guard your hearts and your minds in Christ Jesus.

PRAYER

_____
_____
_____
_____
_____
_____
_____
_____

DEPRESSION

- **Psalm 3:3** But you, LORD, are a shield around me, my glory, the One who lifts my head high.
- **Isaiah 41:10** So do not fear, for I am with you; do not be dismayed, for I am your God. I will strengthen you and help you; I will uphold you with my righteous right hand.
- **1 Peter 5:6-7** Humble yourselves, therefore, under God's mighty hand, that he may lift you up in due time. 7 Cast all your anxiety on him because he cares for you.
- **John 16:33** I have told you these things, so that in me you may have peace. In this world, you will have trouble. But take heart! I have overcome the world

PRAYER

_____
_____
_____
_____
_____
_____
_____

DOUBT

- James 1:6 But when you ask, you must believe and not doubt, because the one who doubts is like a wave of the sea, blown and tossed by the wind.
- Matthew 21:21-22 And Jesus answered and said to them, "Truly I say to you, if you have faith and do not doubt, you will not only do what was done to the fig tree but even if you say to this mountain, 'Be taken up and cast into the sea,' it will happen. "And all things you ask in prayer, believing, you will receive." (ESV)
- Psalm 119:147 I rise before dawn and cry for help; I wait for your word.
- Hebrew 11:1 Now faith is the substance of things hoped for, the evidence of things not seen (KJV).

PRAYER

FEAR

- Romans 12:2 Surely God is my salvation; I will trust and not be afraid. The LORD, the LORD himself, is my strength and my defense; he has become my salvation."
- John 14:27 Peace I leave with you; my peace I give you. I do not give to you as the world gives. Do not let your hearts be troubled and do not be afraid.
- 2 Timothy 1:7 For God hath not given us the spirit of fear, but of power, and of love, and of a sound mind (KJV).
- Psalm 23:4 Even though I walk through the darkest valley, I will fear no evil, for you are with me; your rod and your staff, they comfort me.

PRAYER

_____
_____
_____
_____
_____
_____
_____
_____

HOPE

- **Romans 15:13** May the God of hope fill you with all joy and peace in believing, so that by the power of the Holy Spirit you may abound in hope (ESV).
- **Psalm 39:7** and now, O Lord, for what do I wait? My hope is in you (ESV).
- **Isaiah 40:31** but those who hope in the LORD will renew their strength. They will soar on wings like eagles; they will run and not grow weary, they will walk and not be faint.
- **Psalm 130:5** I wait for the Lord, my soul waits, and in his word, I hope (ESV);

PRAYER

_____

_____

_____

_____

_____

_____

_____

LONELINESS

- Matthew 11:28 Come to me, all you who labor and are heavy laden, and I will give you rest (ESV).
- 2 Thessalonians 3:16 Now may the Lord of peace himself give you peace at all times and every way. The Lord be with all of you.
- Deuteronomy 31:8 The Lord himself goes before you and will be with you; he will never leave you nor forsake you. Do not be afraid; do not be discouraged.
- Psalm 16:11 You will show me the path of life; in your presence is fullness of joy; at Your right hand are pleasure forevermore.

PRAYER

_____

_____

_____

_____

_____

_____

_____

_____

Worry

- Luke 12:22 Then Jesus said to His disciples: "Therefore I tell you, do not worry about your life, what you will eat; or about your body, what you will wear.
- Matthew 6:33-34 But seek first His kingdom and his righteousness, and all things will be given to you as well. Therefore do not worry about tomorrow, for tomorrow will worry about itself. Each day has enough trouble of its own.
- Proverbs 3:5-6 Trust in the Lord with all your heart and lean not on your own understanding; in all your ways submit to him, and he will make your paths straight.
- Colossians 3:15 Let the peace of Christ rule in your hearts, since as members of one body you were called to peace. And be thankful.

Prayer

ABOUT THE AUTHOR

Paige Tucker is an entrepreneur and owner of Be Your Best You LLC, a consulting agency with a mission to transform communities through empowering individuals and organizations to be their best mentally, physically, financially, and logistically. Created to satisfy Paige's many passions, she hopes that through the work of Be Your Best You LLC she is able to inspire others to become the best versions of themselves.

Born in North Charleston, SC and raised in Birmingham, AL, Paige has wanted to be an author her entire life. She is the oldest of 8 children. Raised by her mother, and later by her maternal grandparents, Paige found solace in writing at a very young age. She has owned several journals throughout her life. Paige believes that she expresses herself better in writing than she does verbally. As an avid reader, she felt compelled to write her own story one day.

Paige holds a degree in Medicine, Healthy & Society from Vanderbilt University in Nashville, TN and a Masters of Human Services from Southeastern University in Lakeland, Fl. Paige is very dedicated to her community and uses her voice to advocate for change. She also is a certified Adult and Youth Mental Health First Aid instructor which has allowed her to spread awareness and education to end the stigma associated with mental illness. She is also the co-creator and co-host of a web show called Complex Chemistry with a mission to promote healing and healthy relationships through conscious conversations.

In her free time, Paige spends her time volunteering in her community through various organizations, mentoring youth, reading, cooking, and spending time with friends and family. She most of all loves traveling. She enjoys seeing the world and immersing herself in different cultures.

Learn more about the work Paige is doing at www.beyourbestyoullc.com

Made in the USA
Coppell, TX
16 December 2019